Dedicated to all of the sporty girls out there.
- P.E.

The Sporty Little Spider

By Patricia Esperon

Illustrated By Amy Klein

The Sporty Little Spider Dyslexic Edition

Text©2020 Patricia Suzanne Esperon

Cover and Interior Art©2020 Amy Klein

All rights reserved, including the right to reproduce this book or portions thereof in any form whatsoever.
For information, e-mail the publisher at:

patriciaesperon@yahoo.com

Revised Edition

ISBN
Hardcover: 978-1-64372-079-1
Softcover: 978-1-64372-080-7

The Sporty Little Spider strapped on her water skis.
She was splashed by a wave, and fell to her knees.

She held onto the rope attached to the motor boat, Then the **S**porty **L**ittle **S**pider kept herself afloat.

The **S**porty **L**ittle **S**pider sat down on the chair lift.

She rode down the slope, right into a snowdrift.

The snow blew away, and when she could see, The Sporty Little Spider went boarding through the trees.

The Sporty Little Spider looked up at the rock wall.

She tried to make it up, and took a little fall.

She scouted all around, and found a better way, then The **S**porty **L**ittle **S**pider climbed up all the way.

The **S**porty **L**ittle **S**pider peddled up the biking trail.
Out jumped a bear, and off her bike she sailed.

The bear ran away, and when the trail was clear, The Sporty Little Spider rode on without a fear.

The **S**porty **L**ittle **S**pider pushed off of the dock. **S**he began to paddle down, and got stuck on a rock.

She used all her strength, and got the kayak free, then The Sporty Little Spider paddled happy as could be.

The **S**porty **L**ittle **S**pider climbed up the mountainside. She hurried to the edge, ready to hang glide.

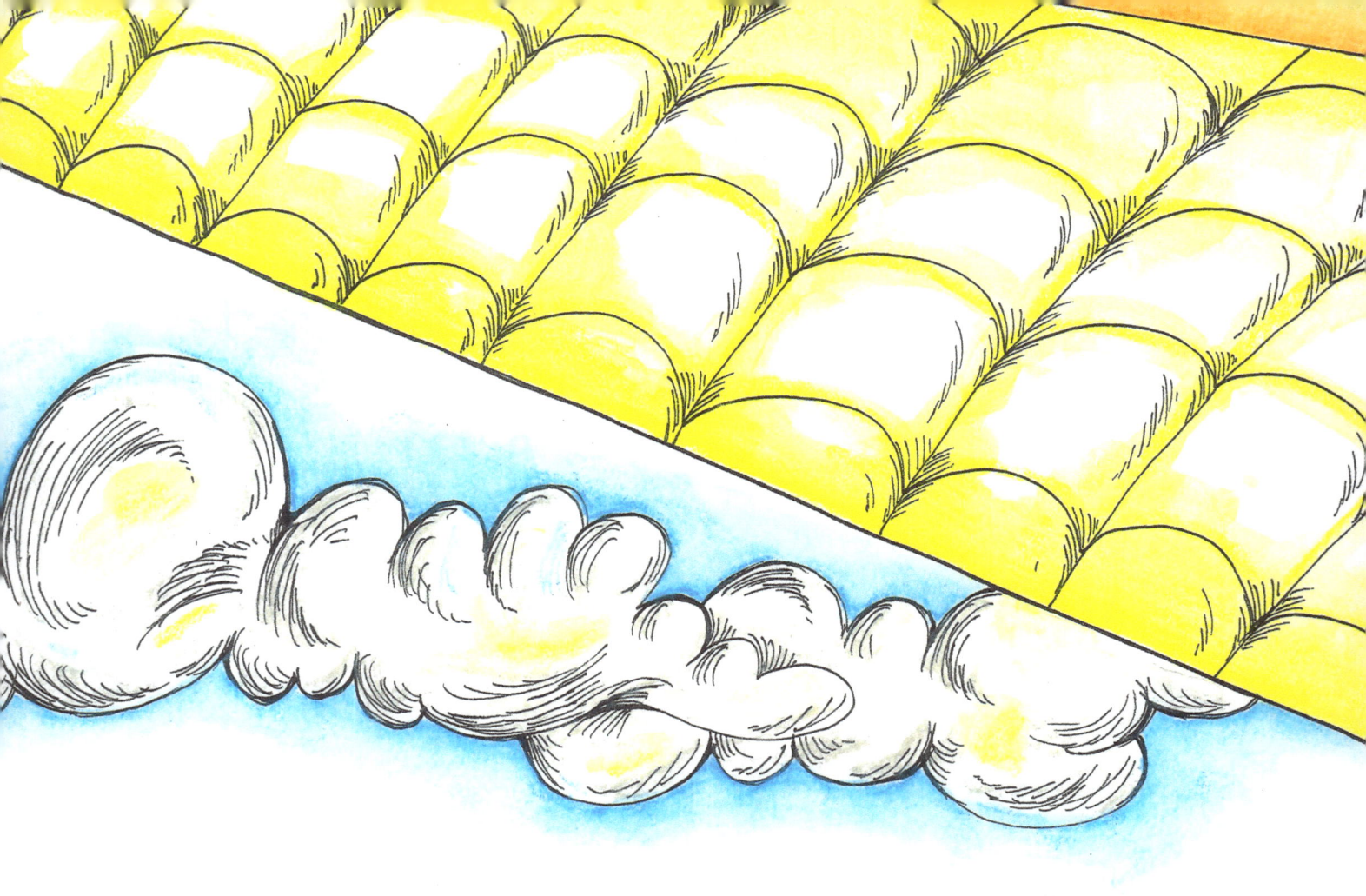

She took a deep breath, and next she closed her eyes. Then the **S**porty **L**ittle **S**pider floated up into the sky.

Author
Patricia Esperon

Award-winning essayist and author Patricia Esperon has just published her first children's book. She holds her master's degree in clinical counseling and her certificate in horticultural therapy. She is passionate about counseling clients in a garden or greenhouse setting and teaching about gardening.

Patricia was inspired to write her stories by her two sons. She enjoys writing and reading. She lives in the Vail Valley of Colorado where she engages in outdoor athletic activities when she is not immersed in gardening. Originally from Peoria, Illinois, she still feels connected to her Midwestern roots.

Illustrator
Amy Klein

Art has always been my passion! My art has taken the form of illustration, toy design, live event painting, mural installation, fashion and textile design, street chalk art, cake decorating and more. When I'm not in my studio I love to be outdoors with my family enjoying my beautiful state of Colorado - hiking, biking, skiing and being inspired by nature!

What is Dyslexie Font?

Each letter is given its own identity making it easier for people with dyslexia to be more successful at reading.

The Dyslexie font:
1. Makes letters easier to distinguish
2. Offers more ease, regularity and joy in reading
3. Enables you to read with less effort
4. Gives your self-esteem a boost
5. Can be used anywhere, anytime and on (almost) every device
6. Does not require additional software or programs
7. Offers the simplest and most effective reading support

The Dyslexie font is specially designed for people with dyslexia, in order to make reading easier – and more fun. During the design process, all basic typography rules and standards were ignored. Readability and specific characteristics of dyslexia are used as guidelines for the design.

Graphic designer Christian Boer created a dyslexic-friendly font to make reading easier for people with dyslexia, like himself.

"Traditional fonts are designed solely from an aesthetic point of view," Boer writes on his website, "which means they often have characteristics that make characters difficult to recognize for people with dyslexia. Oftentimes, the letters of a word are confused, turned around or jumbled up because they look too similar."

Designed to make reading clearer and more enjoyable for people with dyslexia, Dyslexie uses heavy base lines, alternating stick and tail lengths, larger openings, and semicursive slants to ensure that each character has a unique and more easily recognizable form.

Our books are not just for children to enjoy, they are also for adults who have dyslexia who want the experience of reading to the children in their lives.

Learn more and get the font for your digital devices at
www.dyslexiefont.com

Get books in Dyslexie Font at: www.mcp-store.com

4 I can read to you — Engaging stories, longer sentences, and language play for developing readers who still need some help.